WHAT THEY'RE SAYING ABOUT

THE BURDEN

"This is an astonishing work. A jeremiad of relentless spiritual force and prophetic potency. *The Burden* has the power of Jeremiah's message mystically fused with the Muse of T. S. Eliot. It shows the *Heiliger Geist* ripping the *Zeitgeist* to shreds, the Holy Spirit excoriating and exorcising the Spirit of the Age. It speaks with the righteous anger that Christ poured forth on the money changers in the temple. It is a blowtorch in the dark. *The Burden* is light! It will enlighten your life and lighten your burdens."

JOSEPH PEARCE
Writer-in-Residence, Thomas More College, New Hampshire

"With swirling and sobering language that sears the heart, awakens the mind, and cries out to heaven, *The Burden* is a strange and marvelous book of poetic prophecy for our perilous times. Paul Thigpen has gathered ideas and imagery from Sacred Scripture and woven them into his own ominous words of warning. *The Burden* thunders God's righteous rage in a tumultuous storm of judgment mixed with the innocence and poignancy of a Father's broken heart.

"This is a crucial call to complacent Christians wandering in the Wasteland to wake up and repent before it's too late."

FR. DWIGHT LONGENECKER
Blogger, broadcaster and author of The Quest for the Creed, Catholicism Pure and Simple, *and* The Gargoyle Code

"*The Burden* is a brilliant work — bold, daring and fabulously engaging. It is a gift for our sated age. It offers a concentrated dose of profound insights into things that have come to pass and could very well portend for the future. As Paul Thigpen is a sober and clear-thinking Catholic author, I have to conclude that this work was inspired by the Holy Spirit. If so, let's hope and pray that this work serves as a clarion call that will stir the hearts of those who slumber and will quicken the steps of those who strongly believe in God's message."

MATTHEW PINTO
Coeditor, The Amazing Grace Series

"*The Burden* echoed in my spirit as though hearing the voice of God. This gripping prophetic declaration is studded with vivid imagery that will move some to repentance and the sure discovery of God's mercy. Others will nervously start looking over their shoulders to double-check whether either judgment or redemption is nigh and nipping at their heels. The keen use of Scripture propels us into the world of the apostles, prophets, and martyrs. It will sober the foolish and bring tears to the wise. This message breathes urgency and demands response, maybe revival. It might be a nation-changer if it first explodes as a Church-changer."

AL KRESTA
President and CEO of Ave Maria Communications

"'In the beginning was the Word, and the Word was with God and the Word was God (John 1:1).' At the end there was the Word, and the Word was with God, and the Word is God. Paul Thigpen's *Burden* is the voice of that Word spoken in time, to our time, from beyond the reaches of time. It is a voice so searing and luminescent that you know from the first sound it can only belong to I AM. And the word this I AM has for men in our age is most terrifying precisely because it is likely less a warning to lost man than an alert to a remnant of what is now underway."

BRIAN J. GAIL
Author of Fatherless, Motherless, *and* Childless (The American Tragedy in Trilogy)

THE BURDEN

THE BURDEN

A WARNING OF THINGS TO COME

PAUL THIGPEN

Sea Star Press
Atlanta

The Burden by Paul Thigpen
Published in the United States by
Sea Star Press
P.O. Box 27
Dawsonville, GA 30534

The Scripture citations contained in this work, unless otherwise noted, are taken from the Catholic Edition of the Revised Standard Version of the Bible, copyright © 1965, 1966 by the Division of Christian Education of the National Council of the Churches of Christ in the United States. Used by permission. All rights reserved. The translation of Proverbs 22:3 is the author's own.

Interior and cover design by Jennifer Bitler.
Cover photo by Eky Studio/Shutterstock.com.

ISBN-13:
978-0615780436

ISBN-10:
0615780431

Visit *The Burden* website at www.TheBurdenTheBook.com.

For my dear friend
Jeff
A better man, I've never known
A better friend, no man could ask for

CONTENTS

With gratitude to all who graciously agreed to review the manuscript and confirmed that it must be published. You know who you are.

And the LORD answered me,
"Write the vision,
make it plain upon tablets,
so he may run who reads it."
HABAKKUK 2:2

Those who are prudent see danger
and hide themselves;
but the naïve keep going
and suffer for it.
PROVERBS 22:3

We must work the works of Him who sent Me while it is day;
night comes, when no one can work.
JOHN 9:4

The Burden Bearer

I am no prophet, nor a prophet's son; but ...
the Lord said to me, "Go, prophesy to my people Israel."
AMOS 8:14–15

When people say, "There is peace and security," then sudden
destruction will come upon them as labor pains come upon a
woman with child, and there will be no escape. ... So then let us not
sleep, as others do, but let us keep awake and be sober.
1 THESSALONIANS 5:2–3, 6

"For I the Lord do not change. ... Return to Me,
and I will return to you."
MALACHI 3:6–7

hen the prophets of ancient Israel and Judah declared to the people a message from God, they often spoke of it as a "burden" to be delivered. The image suggests that the message weighed heavily on them, and if the weight was to be lifted, it had to be passed on.

This little book delivers its author's Burden, a report of what he has seen and heard. He hopes to pass it on to as many as will receive it. Its urgent message requires at least a few introductory remarks.

Some who have read the book say that it reads like poetry or prophecy. But the author claims to be neither a poet nor a prophet. Since early childhood, he has pondered biblical prophetic literature, and in delivering his burden, he has taken as his models those inspired poet-prophets of old. We should not be surprised, then, if the thunder of their oracles echoes in what he has to say.

No doubt some will call the Burden bearer a fool, a charge he does not deny. If they are right, he hopes to be a fool for God, for "the foolishness of God is wiser than men" (1 Corinthians 1:25). Time will tell.

So what exactly is the Burden that is delivered here?

First we should note that it is not a prediction, nor even a calculation, that certain scriptural prophecies are being uniquely fulfilled in our day. Such an endeavor, in generations past as well as present, too often leads to misery. "It is not for [us] to know the times or seasons which the Father has fixed by His own authority" (Acts 1:7). In any case, most of the prophetic Old Testament passages quoted here were already fulfilled long ago in the history of the ancient Near East.

At the same time, the author makes no claims for the kinds of private revelation that come as supernatural visions or locutions. Yet he does believe that this Burden came to him from God, who helped him express it as he struggled mightily to find the right words to describe what he had received. Even so, he readily admits that his expression is inadequate and may be otherwise flawed. Let the reader discern.

So why was the Burden given? It is a warning and a call to repentance.

"Do not be deceived," the Apostle Paul tells us. "God is not mocked, for whatever a man sows, that he will also reap" (Galatians 6:7).

We are a generation of mockers, and we face a calamitous harvest. We seem bent on repeating the folly of God's people in ancient times: "They sow the wind, and they shall reap the whirlwind" (Hosea 8:7). Spiritually, socially, politically, economically, the fierce consequences of our sin whirl around us today and threaten us with catastrophe. The storm clouds gather; the thunder rumbles; the darkness descends.

While the tempest approaches, many are asleep. Others sense danger in the air but are uncertain of its source and scope. Perhaps these words can rouse the sleepers and clarify the danger.

The author insists that we are seeing today a repetition of the historical pattern so vividly presented in biblical prophecy, an echo of events that took place long ago. God does not change. His ultimate response to sinful nations — merciful but terrifying chastisement — is universal and timeless. Our recent history invites, perhaps demands, such chastisement in our generation. And that is what the Burden is all about.

For this reason, we do well to study the prophetic texts of Scripture, to ponder how we too have courted destruction by our rejection of God, and to consider how to mend our ways before it is too late. The biblical passages quoted in this book provide a good place to begin such fruitful study. If some readers should conclude that what the author has written is of no value, they can still profit from reading these scriptural texts. The texts are juxtaposed in a way that allows them to shed considerable light on one another.

In addition, the book includes an index of scriptural allusions and parallels, following the main text. These allusions and parallels reveal the biblical fabric of the author's thought and expression. They are more than eight hundred in number, allowing for further and deeper study of related biblical passages.

Which particular contemporary realities are examined here in the light of Scripture? Readers will not find it difficult to identify most of them, despite the highly figurative language employed to describe them.

Nevertheless, at least a few passages will read as if written in a code that must be broken. In this way as well, the author has followed the example of biblical prophecy; and as with the parables of Our Lord, such puzzling pronouncements invite the audience to wrestle earnestly with what has been said — a labor that can lead to unexpected insights.

We should note that, again following the model of prophecy in Scripture, these pages offer spiritual and social commentary joined to dire predictions of calamity (though without time frames). Some of these predictions, such as those describing the tribulations leading to the Last Judgment, will be familiar to many. They have been made certain by the words of Our Lord, though we must trust them to Heaven's timetable.

Other predictions, such as economic collapse, will come as no surprise to readers who are following current events, even to those of no particular religious faith. They seem to be inevitable, short of a global miracle.

Still other passages in the book, however, speak of impending events that are not at all obvious. Are such warnings presented as guaranteed predictions?

One overarching theme throughout biblical prophecy is God's mercy, expressed in His willingness to turn away catastrophe if His people repent. In the Book of Jonah we find that even when a divine prophecy predicted certain destruction, without any conditions stated, repentance on the part of the people (and a notoriously wicked people at that) prompted God to withhold chastisement. (See Jonah 3:4–10.)

Given that precedent, we can safely say this much: Even if the author has accurately expressed a Burden that God has given him, most of the future events described in these pages are conditional. If we turn from our evil ways, we have hope of avoiding the desolation that is threatened.

Still, the burning question remains: Will we turn?

Paul Thigpen
February 13, 2013
Ash Wednesday

I.

THE VOICE

A voice says, "Cry!"
And I said, "What shall I cry?"
All flesh is grass,
and all its beauty is like the flower of the field.
The grass withers, the flower fades,
when the breath of the LORD blows upon it;
surely the people is grass.
The grass withers, the flower fades;
but the word of our God will stand forever.
ISAIAH 40:6–8

The appointed time has grown very short. ... For the form of this
world is passing away.
1 CORINTHIANS 7:29, 31

But the day of the LORD will come like a thief, and then the heavens
will pass away with a loud noise, and the elements will be dissolved
with fire, and the earth and the works that are upon it will be burned
up. Since all these things are thus to be dissolved, what sort of persons
ought you to be in lives of holiness and godliness, waiting for and
hastening the coming of the day of God ...
2 PETER 3:10–12

*I*n the silence of the night,
a still, small Voice came whispering;
in the tumult of the day,
a thundering Cry,
like the sound of many waters:

"You must not remain silent!
You must write what I tell you."

So I asked, trembling,
"What words do You give me?"
And the answer came swift and sure: 10

"The Day of Reckoning approaches;
the Hour of Judgment draws near.
Warn this people;
wake this nation;
call them to conversion;
arouse them to repentance.

"If they listen and return to Me,
they will be saved.
But if they scorn Me,
no one can rescue them."   20

I waited, wondering:
Are these mere imaginings,
long-felt laments
of a world-weary heart?
But the Burden has burgeoned;
I can no longer bear it.
With each passing day
the weight increases,
like a child in the womb,
stirring and kicking,   30
demanding delivery.

Hear now the Burden:

All flesh is grass.
He blesses, we flourish;

He curses, we wither.
His Word alone lasts.

This world is passing,
its butterfly glories
emerging in morning,
splendid at midday,   40
dead at dusk.

I soared to the heavens
and looked down below.
Earth had stopped spinning;
time had ceased flowing;
all was ashes,
ashes and smoke.

Each empire was dust;
each idol, a vapor.
Houses and lands,   50
toys and trifles,
vanished, forgotten.

All flesh is grass.
He blesses, we flourish;
He curses, we wither.
His Word alone lasts.

II.

THE EAGLE

Ah, sinful nation,
a people laden with iniquity,
offspring of evildoers,
sons who deal corruptly!
They have forsaken the LORD,
they have despised the Holy One of Israel,
they are utterly estranged.
Why will you still be smitten,
that you continue to rebel?
The whole head is sick,
and the whole heart faint.
ISAIAH 1:4–6

I will make them a horror to all the kingdoms of the earth,
to be a reproach, a byword, a taunt, and a curse
in all the places where I shall drive them.
And I will send sword, famine, and pestilence upon them,
until they shall be utterly destroyed
from the land which I gave to them and their fathers.
JEREMIAH 24:9–10

I looked to the sky,
and behold, an Eagle,
once young and strong,
now old, weak, and weary.
She no longer soars
or looks to the Sun;
the radiance dazzles
so she closes her eyes
or casts her glances below,
seeking a place to hide.

She folds her wings and dozes
as her enemies advance.
Her rivals sail past her;
her weakened friends fail her;
her fledglings refuse to fly.

The Voice spoke:

"Not age alone has brought you to this state:
You are young among your sisters.
But a sickness unto death saps your strength;
a poison you have sipped leeches out your life;
an arsenic of arrogance runs cold in your veins.

"When I first hatched you in the Sunlight
I saved you from the predators;
I gave you gifts unequalled.
You grew in strength and beauty
and all your sisters marveled
at the freedom of your flight.

"Again and again you flew astray,
yet I was with you;
I never ceased to feed you,
to protect you,
to sustain you,
to call you back to the place
I had prepared for you.

"But now you have ignored Me,
deserted Me,

60

70

80

90

forgotten Me.
Your full belly has deceived you:
No longer do you seek Me.

"If even for a moment
I should withdraw My hand,
you would starve and collapse.
Yet you refuse to return to Me
even the leftover crumbs   100
of your abundance.

"If even once
I should look away from you,
you would return to the dust
from which you came.
Yet you turn your back on Me,
chasing after grubs.

"I call you in the Wind,
but you are deaf.
I beckon you in the Sunlight,   110
but you are blind.

"I send the storms to rouse you
from your dreamless sleep,
but you will not awaken,
you will not arise:
Your slumber foreshadows
your grave.

"Your nest is falling apart,
a fierce free-for-all of feathers.
Your children riot and revolt,   120
and when at last they turn against you
they will tear you wing from breast
until you give up the ghost,
as each one flees
with a portion of your corpse.

"Then, when you are gone,
the circling vultures will take your place
and freedom's face will be forgotten."

III.

THE CHILDREN

These have chosen their own ways,
and their soul delights in their abominations;
I also will choose affliction for them,
and bring their fears upon them;
because, when I called, no one answered,
when I spoke, they did not listen;
but they did what was evil in my eyes,
and chose that in which I did not delight.
ISAIAH 66:3-4

A voice was heard in Ramah,
wailing and loud lamentation,
Rachel weeping for her children;
she refused to be consoled,
because they were no more.
MATTHEW 2:18

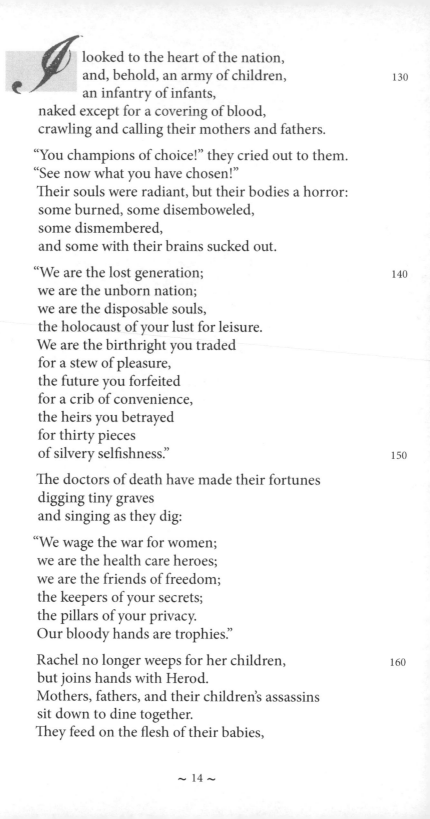

I looked to the heart of the nation,
and, behold, an army of children, 130
an infantry of infants,
naked except for a covering of blood,
crawling and calling their mothers and fathers.

"You champions of choice!" they cried out to them.
"See now what you have chosen!"
Their souls were radiant, but their bodies a horror:
some burned, some disemboweled,
some dismembered,
and some with their brains sucked out.

"We are the lost generation; 140
we are the unborn nation;
we are the disposable souls,
the holocaust of your lust for leisure.
We are the birthright you traded
for a stew of pleasure,
the future you forfeited
for a crib of convenience,
the heirs you betrayed
for thirty pieces
of silvery selfishness." 150

The doctors of death have made their fortunes
digging tiny graves
and singing as they dig:

"We wage the war for women;
we are the health care heroes;
we are the friends of freedom;
the keepers of your secrets;
the pillars of your privacy.
Our bloody hands are trophies."

Rachel no longer weeps for her children, 160
but joins hands with Herod.
Mothers, fathers, and their children's assassins
sit down to dine together.
They feed on the flesh of their babies,

and wipe their mouths, and say,
"We have done nothing wrong."

While all along, the multitudes
pass by and look the other way,
busy with their banalities,
preoccupied with their pleasantries,   170
complacent in their comfort.

"But now," the Voice declares,
"comes the day of My choosing.
It is not penalty enough
for your homes to be empty of play,
your houses bereft of laughter,
your last days alone and abandoned.
These sorrows you have brought upon yourselves.
But for the lifeblood of the little ones
I will surely require a reckoning.   180

"I choose to rain upon you
fire and fury,
frost and famine.
I will flood your fields with blood,
engulf your cities in flame.
The winds and waters
will bear My judgment,
poison of your own creation.

"I will send the Death Angel among you,
with no hope of a Passover to spare you.   190
You have sacrificed the little lambs without remorse;
now the blood on your doorposts will condemn you.
Your wickedness has leavened the whole lump,
and your houses are filled with unclean bread.

"You will flee from Pharaoh,
but you will not escape;
you will seek dry passage,
but the waters will turn you back.
His chariots are drawn
by the Dragon, the Bear, and the Jackal,   200

and his chariots will crush you.
The sea of false promises
in which you had placed your hope
will be red with your blood."

The children cry out, "How long, O Lord?
How long before Your judgment
stays the hand and stills the voice
of our murderers and their accomplices?"

And the Voice answers,
"That Day is only a heartbeat away."   210

IV.

THE COLLAPSE

Woe to you who are rich, for you have received your consolation.
Woe to you who are full now, for you shall hunger.
LUKE 6:24–25

He who is slack in his work is a brother to him who destroys.
PROVERBS 18:9

The rich rules over the poor, and the borrower
is the slave of the lender.
PROVERBS 22:7

The city of chaos is broken down, every house is shut up
so that none can enter. Desolation is left in the city, the gates are
battered into ruins.
ISAIAH 24:10

Therefore thus says the LORD God …
"I will break down the wall
that you have daubed with whitewash,
and bring it down to the ground,
so that its foundation will be laid bare;
when it falls, you shall perish in the midst of it;
and you shall know that I am the LORD."
EZEKIEL 13:13–14

A foolish man … built his house upon the sand; and the rain fell, and
the floods came, and the winds blew and beat against that house, and
it fell; and great was the fall of it.
MATTHEW 7:26–27

Woe to those
who heap up treasure
by grinding the poor:
wringing blood from their brothers,
tears from their sisters,
neglecting their neighbors.
Their gilded calf is lead;
it will poison and plummet.

Woe to those
who refuse to work,   220
who excuse their sloth,
who drink the sweat
of their neighbor's brow
and call it sweet.
Derelicts of deceit,
their poverty is pretense.
Perpetually dependent,
they feel no shame.

Woe to those
who pile up loans   230
they never can repay;
who borrow and pledge
to fill their pockets
and chase their fantasies.
They crush their children
with debt.

Woe to those
who pull the strings,
who fix the scales,
who call the shots   240
from behind the curtain:
They have a bull by the horns;
they have a bear by the tail.
The beast will turn
to devour them.

They have traded
goods for ciphers,

substance for appearance,
community for commodity,
the fruits of labor   250
for the plunder of schemes.

In a moment, their world will collapse:
foundation of sand,
washed to the sea;
bubble of glass,
shattered in shards.

The wrath of the Sun
will flash, will crash
their calculations,
lay waste their walled street,   260
dissolve their deceptions.

The poor, as always, will bear the brunt,
but none can dodge the lightning:
Their coins will be slugs,
their bills will be trash,
their savings will be ashes.

The streets will be void of traffic;
the markets vacant and silent,
except for the weeping.
As the teeming towers empty out,   270
far away the fertile fields will rot.
The foot will be lame
and the hand will have no way
to reach the mouth.

Mothers will fight for a cup of milk;
fathers will steal for a loaf of bread;
children will cry for a crumb.

The rich will be stripped;
the poor will be fodder;
the wicked will prey on the innocent   280
and devour one another
with none to protect or defend.

The prodigals who traded
prudence for pleasure
will envy the swine their slop.
They will have no home
where they can return.
They will have no father
awaiting them,
no robe, no ring,   290
no fatted calf.

Those who have cuddled up
to the great nanny goat
to suck her teats perpetually,
kids who never grow up,
will hunger and riot
when her milk dries up,
will starve when she dies,
will turn on one another
and gorge themselves   300
on blood instead.

The façade of civilization falls;
instead of citizens,
criminals and cannibals
in a cauldron of chaos.

Those who have watered their souls,
fertilized their spirits,
deepened their roots of faith
will survive the storm;
but those with shallow roots will fall;   310
the gales will uproot them,
the floods will sweep them away.

V.

THE BABBLERS

Wise men lay up knowledge,
but the babbling of a fool brings ruin near. ...
When words are many, transgression is not lacking,
but he who restrains his lips is prudent. ...
The mouth of the righteous brings forth wisdom,
but the perverse tongue will be cut off.
The lips of the righteous know what is acceptable,
but the mouth of the wicked, what is perverse.
PROVERBS 10:14, 19, 31–32

Woe to those who call evil good and good evil,
who put darkness for light, and light for darkness,
who put bitter for sweet, and sweet for bitter!
Woe to those who are wise in their own eyes,
and shrewd in their own sight! ...
For truth has fallen in the public squares,
and uprightness cannot enter.
Truth is lacking,
and he who departs from evil
makes himself a prey.
ISAIAH 5:20–21; 59:14–15

Let the lying lips be dumb,
which speak insolently against the righteous
in pride and contempt.
PROVERBS 31:18

Woe to the talking heads with empty chests,
fools posing as magi,
blind leading the blind
into ditches they themselves have dug.
They think to dazzle the masses
with a feigned raiment of wisdom;
but clear-eyed children cry aloud:
"The commentators have no clothes!"   320

Anchors without weight,
foamy flotsam floating
on every fickle wave of feeling;
in place of fairness, fawning.
Their compass is lost;
they drift in treacherous waters.
Their clock is shattered;
they think the dusk is dawn.
Their telescope is foggy;
they cannot see what lies ahead;   330
they steer upon the reefs.

Woe to the whisperers of wickedness,
the hydra of a hundred heads,
spewing bright venom into homes
where parents lap up the poison
and children are sickened
by the noxious fumes.

They scatter scorpions,
they sow serpents,
vipers of violence,   340
vermin of vice.

They gorge on filth
and call it honey;
they celebrate shadow
and call it light;
they mock as morons
the devout, the upright.

Vampire clowns,

entertaining while eviscerating;
their victims are laughing too hard 350
to notice the mutilation.

The Voice came thundering:
"You purveyors of perversity:
Do you think I am deaf?
Do you suppose I am amused?
Do you count My patience as approval,
My mercy as indifference?

"Deceiving, you are deceived.
I will no longer delay My wrath:
The Great Quiet now approaches. 360

"In only a moment,
I will hush the hucksters of hell.
I will abolish the airwaves,
cut the cables,
wipe out the wireless words.
I will darken the screens
and silence the speakers.
I will cleanse the atmosphere
of the toxic cloud
that has hovered over the land. 370

"You will eat your words;
you will choke on your vomit;
you will swallow your tongues;
you will gag and fall mute.
You will render account
for every utterance,
and by the words of your mouth
you will be condemned."

VI.

THE EYES

Sheol and Abaddon are never satisfied,
and never satisfied are the eyes of man.
PROVERBS 27:20

The eyes of a fool are on the ends of the earth.
PROVERBS 17:24

The horn ... had eyes and a mouth that spoke great things, and ...
seemed greater than its fellows. As I looked, this horn made war with
the saints, and prevailed over them, until the Ancient of Days came.
DANIEL 7:19, 20 22

For the ruthless shall come to nought and the scoffer cease,
and all who watch to do evil shall be cut off.
ISAIAH 29:20

The eyes of the wicked will fail, all way of escape will be lost to them,
and their hope is to breathe their last.
JOB 11:20

I beheld the earth,
and circled around it, 380
great wheels within wheels,
spinning and covered with eyes;
a dark cherub of electrons,
four-faced and silent
and hidden behind wings.

Voracious for data,
heedless of privacy,
shrouded in secrecy,
its eyes, unblinking, survey the world;
its brain, unsleeping, connects the dots. 390

In bloodless whispers, calm and confident,
it justifies the stealth:

"I search out evil to defend the good.
My net is woven for the wicked.
I am the guardian angel.
I am indispensable.
I am inevitable.
I am godlike.
I AM."

But knowledge is power, 400
and power corrupts,
and absolute power
corrupts absolutely.

The god has become a demon;
the angel has become a spider;
the net has become a web.
All are caught within it;
all are prey for the predator.

Four faces, four masks:
the face of a man, the mask of humane concern; 410
the face of an ox, the mask of a servant;
the face of a lion, the mask of authority;
the face of an eagle, the mask of a patriot.

The spider behind the masks
who spins the web,
who peers through the eyes,
thirsts for power,
covets control.

Those who challenge him
are quickly ensnared and disarmed;   420
the innocent are blamed;
the righteous, defamed;
the watchmen, arrested and silenced.

The demon-idol tolerates no rival;
he gathers the true-God-worshippers
and sinks his fangs into them,
mixing their blood with his venom.

But high above the spider's head
shines a sapphire throne,
where the Voice explodes in fury: 430

"I AM, and there is no other,
from everlasting to everlasting.
You are the creature of a day,
and the night draws near.
The earth is My footstool,
and you are a speck of dust
beneath My feet.

"Because you dared to touch the holy ones,
I will sweep away your web;
one blast of My breath, and it is gone.   440
I will pull off your masks,
blind your eyes with lightning bolts,
cast you in the furnace of My wrath.

"But the righteous shall shine like the sun
and My saints be ablaze with My glory."

VII.

The Idolaters

Your lewdness shall be requited upon you,
and you shall bear the penalty for your sinful idolatry;
and you shall know that I am the LORD.
EZEKIEL 23:49

Put to death therefore what is earthly in you: immorality, impurity,
passion, evil desire, and covetousness, which is idolatry. On account of
these the wrath of God is coming.
COLOSSIANS 3:5-6

And he carried me away in the Spirit into a wilderness, and I saw
a woman sitting on a scarlet beast which was full of blasphemous
names, and it had seven heads and ten horns. The woman was
arrayed in purple and scarlet, and bedecked with gold and jewels and
pearls, holding in her hand a golden cup full of abominations and
the impurities of her fornication; and on her forehead was written a
name of mystery: "Babylon the great, mother of harlots and of earth's
abominations." And I saw the woman, drunk with the blood of the
saints and the blood of the martyrs of Jesus.
REVELATION 17:3-6

"Fallen, fallen, is Babylon the great, she who made all nations drink
the wine of her impure passion."
REVELATION 14:8

Little children, keep yourselves from idols.
1 JOHN 5:21

The spirit of the ravenous Harlot
has returned to possess the land.
        Queen of immoralities,
Lady of licentiousness,
she screams her incantations.   450

She rides upon a multi-headed
beast of many nations
scarlet with lust
and panting to praise her.

In her honor abound
icons of obscenity,
omnipresent images,
in homes, in shops, on city streets:
emblems of obsession.
Her devotees flatter her by imitation: 460
They deck themselves in her fashions;
their language mimics her lewdness.
At every hour she is worshipped,
while Chastity is scorned.

A host of her cult prostitutes,
male and female,
male and male,
female and female,
couple in barren embrace,
burning with lust,   470
heedless of love.

A sly merchant and marketer,
she exports her wine throughout the world,
and the world pays dearly for the drink.
Those who share her cup become her slaves:
The draught is drugged.

The deadly Dominatrix
has neither patience nor pity.
In the name of tolerance,
she demands their submission,   480
commands their kiss,

and spurs her steed
to trample all
who refuse her chalice.
She mixcs their blood with her wine
and delights in the taste of tyranny.

Her reign is coming to an end.
Addicted adorers, degraded, despairing,
will desert her temples in desperation,
and those who remain
will die in the desert
of demented devotion.

490

Her spells will be broken,
her idols forgotten,
her power dissolved,
when Judgment sweeps away her shrines
and brutal Survival becomes the new tyrant.

VIII.

THE PRINCELINGS

I will make boys their princes,
and infants shall rule over them.
And the people will oppress one another,
every man his fellow
and every man his neighbor;
the youth will be insolent to the elder,
and the base fellow to the honorable. ...
O My people, your leaders mislead you,
and confuse the course of your paths.
The LORD has taken His place to contend,
He stands to judge His people.
The LORD enters into judgment
with the elders and princes of His people.
ISAIAH 3:4–5, 12–14

For My people are foolish,
they know Me not;
they are stupid children,
they have no understanding.
They are skilled in doing evil,
but how to do good they know not.
JEREMIAH 4:22

But to what shall I compare this generation? It is like children sitting
in the marketplaces and calling to their playmates ...
MATTHEW 11:16

I looked out across the land
and peered into the halls of the rulers,
the chambers of the judges,   500
the backrooms of the powerbrokers.
I searched for elders;
but only a few remained.

I sought out kings and queens
but found instead toddlers:
the preening princeling,
the primping princess,
spoiled fruit of a generation
of little lost babes
who never grew up.   510

They feel but cannot think;
they take but cannot give;
they clutch but cannot hold;
they scatter but cannot gather;
they ride but cannot walk.

The children are running the orphanage
and while they play their games,
recite their nursery rhymes,
suck their lollipops,
take their naps,   520
soil their diapers,
the rafters are ablaze;
the roof collapses on them;
the walls fall down around them.

The spirits of their parents weep:
The house they built, preserved,
the home they defended with blood and tears,
falls into ruin beyond repair,
a haunt of wild beasts
who come to plunder.   530

The Voice declares:

"I give you one last chance to grow up.
Suffering will be your schoolmaster;

misery will be your mentor;
pain will press you to come of age,
to lay aside your childish ways.

"But if you refuse,
if you turn again your back on tomorrow
for the sake of indulgence today,
you will be food   540
for the Dragon, the Bear, and the Jackal,
and the cradlesong you have cooed to yourself
will be your last lullaby."

IX.

THE JACKALS

I have laid waste his hill country and left his heritage
to jackals of the desert.
MALACHI 1:3

"I will appoint over them
four kinds of destroyers,"
says the LORD:
the sword to slay,
the dogs to tear,
and the birds of the air
and the beasts of the earth
to devour and destroy.
And I will make them a horror
to all the kingdoms of the earth."
JEREMIAH 15:3–4

All you beasts of the field, come to devour —
all you beasts in the forest.
His watchmen are blind,
they are all without knowledge;
they are all dumb dogs; they cannot bark;
dreaming, lying down, loving to slumber.
The dogs have a mighty appetite,
they never have enough.
The shepherds also have no understanding.
ISAIAH 56:9–11

ut of the eastern desert
the Jackal awakens again
and leaps up, howling.

The Prince of Darkness trained him;
the Lord of the Flies now drives him,
biting his rump:
crazed, arrogant, ravenous, lecherous; 550
snarling, gnashing his teeth;
with blood and blasphemies in his mouth,
and a stained black banner beside him.

Behind him, a host of jackals run, aping him.
They riot, taking hostage the lands they invade;
both sheep and goats fall prey before them.

They reap, but they do not plant;
like locusts they consume and are not sated.
Guests at a feast not of their making,
they come with empty hands and empty heads, 560
darkened hearts and darkened minds,
robbing and reviling their hosts.

They cry, "Peace! Peace!"
but know nothing of peace,
only the suffocating submission of slaves.
Their hearts are steeped in hatred,
their thoughts resound with resentment,
like bullying children, hiding their fears
behind a veil of vehemence.

They peer into their grand delusion, 570
a warped and broken mirror,
to see an army of glorious stallions,
conquering in the name of heaven.

They listen to the clamorous voices in their heads
a demented echo chamber,
and hear a noble call to arms,
the victorious war cry of heaven.

The Day will come

when they are stripped naked of their illusions,
humiliated and confounded,   580
when the world wakes
from the nightmare they inhabit.

The Day will come
when they fall upon the stumbling Block,
and those who embrace the Stone and rise again
will no longer be ashamed.

But that Day is not yet.
Before the Dawn, there comes
a long night in the West,
where the Sun has set in darkness,   590
where the crescent moon has turned to blood,
where the sheep have wandered blindly
into caves for shelter,
where the goats have sullied
the streams with their dung,
where the shepherds have fallen asleep.

X.

THE FLOCK

Give glory to the LORD your God before He brings darkness, before your feet stumble on the twilight mountains, and while you look for light, He turns it into gloom and makes it deep darkness. But if you will not listen, my soul will weep in secret for your pride; my eyes will weep bitterly and run down with tears, because the LORD's flock has been taken captive. ... My people have been lost sheep; their shepherds have led them astray, turning them away on the mountains; from mountain to hill they have gone, they have forgotten their fold. All who found them have devoured them ...
JEREMIAH 13:16–17; 50:6–7

*"Strike the shepherd, that the sheep may be scattered;
I will turn my hand against the little ones.
In the whole land, says the LORD,
two thirds shall be cut off and perish,
and one third shall be left alive.
And I will put this third into the fire,
and refine them as one refines silver,
and test them as gold is tested.
They will call on My name,
and I will answer them."*
ZECHARIAH 13:7–9

*T*he Voice cried out:

"I brought you to this land of refuge:
I made you lie down in green pastures;
I led you beside still waters;   600
I restored your soul.
I laid out paths of righteousness;
goodness and mercy followed you,
a choice flock.

"How quickly you forgot me!
How soon you went astray!
How easily you wandered
from security to vanity,
from vanity to autonomy,
from autonomy to infidelity.   610

"You have trampled the pastures,
contaminated the waters,
poured out your soul
upon the rocks.

"The true shepherds, you ignore;
the hirelings, you follow,
bleating blindly as you go.
You have romped with the goats,
skipped down rabbit trails,
scattered across the hills,   620
chasing your pleasures.

"The aging, sagging ewes,
the rasping, tottering rams,
who have danced to the panpipes
now collapse in exhaustion.

"The little lambs are lost;
the storm is quickly gathering;
the darkness is descending,
the flock is far from home.

"The Lion will stalk them;   630
the Jackal claims the stragglers.

Those who survive the wolf
will be snatched by the vulture;
those who escape the vulture
will fall to the scorpion.

"Some within the fold
are wool-wrapped wolves:
They will cast off their fluffy pretense,
reveal their fangs,
betray the lambs.   640
They will fleece them,
bludgeon them,
to serve their fellows
a grisly feast.

"But the brave who defy the Predator,
who stand their ground in the darkness
and wash their wool in crimson
I will take to the Lamb's own pasture.
He will guide them to living waters;
He will wipe away their tears;   650
and their blood will be seed.

"Out of the killing fields
I will save a remnant of the flock
who cry to Me.
I will give them shepherds,
feed them in secret,
shelter them in my fold,
in the shadow of my Rock.
Through fiery trials
they will be tested and purified.   660

"But those who take My name in vain
to disguise their rebellion
will slither into outer darkness,
with weeping and gnashing of fangs.
I never knew you; depart from Me,
you evildoers."

XI.

THE SHEPHERDS

Wail, you shepherds, and cry, and roll in the ashes, you lords of the flock, for the days of your slaughter and dispersion have come, and you shall fall like choice rams. No refuge will remain for the shepherds, nor escape for the lords of the flock. … For the LORD is despoiling their pasture …
JEREMIAH 25:34–36

Take heed to yourselves and to all the flock, in which the Holy Spirit has made you guardians, to feed the Church of the LORD which He obtained with His own blood. I know that after my departure fierce wolves will come in among you, not sparing the flock; and from among your own selves will arise men speaking perverse things, to draw away the disciples after them. Therefore be alert ….
ACTS 20:28–31

Tend the flock of God that is your charge, not by constraint but willingly, not for shameful gain but eagerly, not as domineering over those in your charge but being examples to the flock. And when the chief Shepherd is manifested you will obtain the unfading crown of glory. … Be sober, be watchful. Your adversary the devil prowls around like a roaring lion, seeking someone to devour. Resist him, firm in your faith, knowing that the same experience of suffering is required of your brotherhood throughout the world. And after you have suffered a little while, the God of all grace, who has called you to His eternal glory in Christ, will Himself restore, establish and strengthen you.
1 PETER 5:2–4, 8–10

*T*he Voice asked:

"What shall I say of the shepherds?

"In the day of deadly confusion
  many have stood firm.
In the dusk of seductive temptation,   670
  many have stayed pure.
In the night of brutal assault
  many have defended the flock.

"But some have forsaken
  the sure path of their fathers.
Wandering by the wayside,
  groping in blindness,
they have plunged into the ravine,
  taking their sheep with them.

"Some have rolled in filth,   680
  soiled themselves,
betrayed their lambs,
  and driven them away.

"Some are but hirelings:
When the Lion attacked,
  they threw down their rod,
  laid down their staff,
offered up the lambs
  as the price for their own security.

"In the day of My wrath   690
  the hearts of the shepherds
will be revealed,
  their destinies displayed.

"The wanderers will perish.
The filthy will rot.
The hirelings will die
  as slaves to those who hired them.

"But as for the faithful shepherds,
  the pure, the courageous,
who lay down their lives in the valley: 700

I Myself will walk beside them
through the shadow of death,
and they will dwell with Me
in My house forever,
crowned with glory
that will never dim."

XII.

THE ROCK

And Jesus answered him, "Blessed are you, Simon Bar-Jona! For flesh and blood has not revealed this to you, but My Father who is in heaven. And I tell you, you are Peter, and on this rock I will build my Church, and the gates of Hades shall not prevail against it. I will give you the keys of the kingdom of heaven, and whatever you bind on earth shall be bound in heaven, and whatever you loose on earth shall be loosed in heaven."
MATTHEW 16:18–19

"Simon, Simon, behold, Satan demanded to have you, that he might sift you like wheat, but I have prayed for you that your faith may not fail; and when you have turned again, strengthen your brethren."
LUKE 22:31–32

Jesus said to him, "Feed My sheep. Truly, truly, I say to you, when you were young you girded yourself and walked where you would; but when you are old, you will stretch out your hands, and another will gird you and carry you where you do not wish to go." This He said to show by what death he was to glorify God. And after this He said to him, "Follow me."
JOHN 21:17–19

The rats scamper
under Peter's chair.
The wolves are snarling,
the jackals, howling,   710
the bulls surround,
the Lion paces,
the oxen show their horns.

The Voice calls:

"Peter!
The storms around you
seek to enter your heart:
whirlwind of confusion,
deluge of doubt,
thunder of fear.   720
The flood sweeps in
and dashes against the Rock.

"But I AM your refuge in the tempest.
I AM your stillness in the tumult.
When you have done all, stand fast in Me.

"Turn and strengthen your brothers,
forgive those who betray you,
then come, follow Me
on the Way of Sorrows.

"The gates of hell will not prevail   730
but when you are old
they will seize you;
they will stare and gloat;
they will mock and scorn.
They will rend your raiment
and cast lots for your house.
They will stretch out your arms,
pierce your hands and feet,
lay you in the dust of death.

"When it seems you are abandoned,   740
I AM with you, I will embrace you,
as I embraced My dying Son.

And as the earth fades, as your eyes close,
you will see the darkness rent,
and the heavens opened;
I will clothe you with the Morning Star."

XIII.

THE NATIONS

The nations shall see and be ashamed of all their might;
they shall lay their hands on their mouths;
their ears shall be deaf;
they shall lick the dust like a serpent,
like the crawling things of the earth;
they shall come trembling out of their strongholds,
they shall turn in dread to the LORD our God.
MICAH 7:16-17

Behold, the LORD will lay waste the earth and make it desolate, and
He will twist its surface and scatter its inhabitants. ... The heavens
languish together with the earth. The earth lies polluted under its
inhabitants; for they have transgressed the laws, violated the statutes,
broken the everlasting covenant. Therefore a curse devours the earth,
and its inhabitants suffer for their guilt. Therefore the inhabitants
of the earth are scorched, and few men are left. ... The mirth of the
timbrels is stilled, the noise of the jubilant has ceased, the mirth of
the lyre is stilled. ... All joy has reached its eventide; the gladness of
the earth is banished. ... For the windows of heaven are opened, and
the foundations of the earth tremble. The earth is utterly broken, the
earth is rent asunder, the earth is violently shaken. ... Its transgression
lies heavy upon it, and it falls, and will not rise again.
ISAIAH 24:1, 4-6, 8, 11, 18-20

*T*he torch descends,
its tail a dragon's breath.
All nations shall see it
and know the end is near.   750
The ghosts of their ancestors
will be granted a visitation
to warn of the woes approaching:

Wars and rumors of wars;
blinding mushrooms;
rain of flame;
to breathe is to die.

Earthquakes and floods;
plague and pestilence;
horror by day;   760
terror by night;
ashes to ashes;
dust to dust.

All who mocked will mourn;
all who scorned will sorrow,
their shouts of exultation
dissolved in shameful whimpers.
Those who danced will languish;
those who sang will suffocate.

The Voice declares to the nations: 770

"All these long ages
My bow has shielded you from the flood;
but I gave no promise to hold back this sea of fire.

"All nations will bear the load of their sins
and drink the cup of My anger.
No people will escape My wrath;
no tribe will elude My chastisement;
none except the dead.
The living will envy the departed;
and call them blessed.   780

"But to those who are faithful unto death,

from every tribe and tongue, people and nation,
I will give a crown of life."

XIV.

THE WOMAN

And a great sign appeared in heaven,
a woman clothed with the sun,
with the moon under her feet,
and on her head a crown of twelve stars;
she was with child
and she cried out in her pangs of birth,
in anguish for delivery. ...
She brought forth a male child,
one who is to rule all the nations
with a rod of iron ...
REVELATION 12:1-2, 5

I consider that the sufferings of this present time are not worth
comparing with the glory that is to be revealed to us. For the creation
waits with eager longing for the revealing of the sons of God; for the
creation was subjected to futility, not of its own will, but by the will
of Him who subjected it in hope; because the creation itself will be
set free from its bondage to decay and obtain the glorious liberty
of the children of God. We know that the whole creation has been
groaning with labor pains until now, and not only the creation, but
we ourselves, who have the first fruits of the Spirit, groan inwardly as
we wait ...
ROMANS 8:18-23

_T_hen all about me
I heard groaning.
From one end of the firmament
to the other,
a countless host of voices,
crying out in chorus;
agony of men,   790
sympathy of angels,
in holy harmony,
begging for the birth
of the new creation.

The universe was dancing
to the trembling music
of the spheres:
stars and planets swirling;
galaxies in a gambol;
every quark quivering   800
with bright anticipation.

At the heart of the dance
the Woman was enthroned:
stars about her head,
clothed with the Sun,
moon beneath her feet,
Queen Mother of the King
who rules all nations.

Channel of grace to creation,
the Woman sighs with eager longing,   810
interceding for her children,
breaking bonds of long decay.

She sings with stern solemnity
a new magnificat:

"My soul exults in the Lord!
He bares His arms in judgment.
Laughing, He scatters the proud from their Babel,
dissolves their delusion of dominion.

He casts down the mighty from their thrones,
and raises the lowly to share His reign!"   820

Softly now she weeps.
Her tears descend
from stars to sun,
from sun to moon,
from moon to earth,
a tiny globe convulsing, dying,
thirsty for the healing drops.

She watches as the Serpent
rears his head
and through her tears   830
she smiles to know
her Seed, once bruised,
will crush him utterly.

XV.

The Day

The great day of the LORD is near, near and hastening fast; the sound of the day of the LORD is bitter, the mighty man cries aloud there. A day of wrath is that day, a day of distress and anguish, a day of ruin and devastation, a day of darkness and gloom, a day of clouds and thick darkness, a day of trumpet blast and battle cry. ... I will bring distress on men, so that they shall walk like the blind, because they have sinned against the LORD. In the fire of His jealous wrath, all the earth shall be consumed; for a full, yes, sudden end He will make of all the inhabitants of the earth.
ZEPHANIAH 1:14–18

Behold, the day of the LORD comes, cruel, with wrath and fierce anger, to make the earth a desolation and to destroy its sinners from it. For the stars of the heavens and their constellations will not give their light; the sun will be dark at its rising and the moon will not shed its light. I will punish the world for its evil, and the wicked for their iniquity; I will put an end to the pride of the arrogant, and lay low the haughtiness of the ruthless. ... Therefore I will make the heavens tremble, and the earth will be shaken out of its place, at the wrath of the LORD of hosts in the day of His fierce anger.
ISAIAH 13:9–11, 13

"Behold, I am coming soon, bringing My recompense, to repay every one for what he has done. I AM the Alpha and the Omega, the first and the last, the beginning and the end."
REVELATION 22:12

"After all these things are accomplished,"
     says the Voice,
          "when at last the wicked
     have done their worst
     and the hour of darkness
     has come to an end;
     when the world, in mortal illness,   840
     quakes with the death rattle,
     on a day, at an hour
     you cannot know,
     I will descend from heaven
     with the trumpet of triumph,
     piercing black clouds like lightning,
     glorious hosts in My train.

"I will gather the souls from all the ages;
     I will call back their bodies from their graves.
     The earth will yield her captives;   850
     the sea will give up her dead.
     The stars will witness
     the day of My coming,
     the galaxies watch
     as My glory explodes.

"All men will pass before Me,
     naked, known, announced,
     each whisper now shouted,
     each secret revealed.
     I will show them their deeds,   860
     both good and evil,
     like stones dropped in water,
     rippling out to the world.

"They will gaze upon My glory
     as in the mirror of a calm, crystal sea
     and there behold themselves as I see them,
     as they truly are.

"I will uncover at last the vast canvas
     of my age-old masterpiece:
     I have painted all their portraits,   870

a multitude of faces
in history's long landscape
with strokes both light and dark,
hues both bright and dull;
and all is framed by grace.

"I will be vindicated in the eyes of all flesh,
and every knee shall bow, every tongue confess
that I AM Lord."

"Then the furnace of My holiness
will blaze out through the universe,   880
consuming my enemies,
but cleansing my friends,
until they are filled
with the brilliance of My glory."

On that Day,
at the sound of that Voice
the earth will melt,
and the oceans flee away;
the moon will bleed,
the sun will burn out,   890
the stars will plunge
and the heavens curl up
like a crumbling scroll.

Then the Serpent and his brood
will be cast into the lake of fire,
never again to tempt or accuse,
never again to seduce or deceive.
Their smoke will rise forever;
their agony will never sleep.

But the lambs of the Lamb will drink   900
from the springs of Living Water.
The saints of the Most High
will rule with Him,
casting their crowns before the Throne,
singing the new and everlasting song:

"Holy, Holy, Holy

is the Lord God Almighty,
who was, and who is,
and who is to come!"

The Bride at last will behold the Bridegroom; 910
and time will be no more;
she will embrace in final ecstasy
the Alpha and the Omega,
the First and the Last,
the Beginning and the End,
the eternal I AM.

XVI.

The Choice

See that you do not refuse Him who is speaking. For if they did not escape when they refused Him who warned them on earth, much less shall we escape if we reject Him who warns from heaven. His voice then shook the earth; but now He has promised, "Yet once more I will shake not only the earth but also the heaven."... Our God is a consuming fire.
HEBREWS 12:25–26, 29

Seek the LORD while He may be found, call upon Him while He is near; let the wicked forsake his way, and the unrighteous man his thoughts; let him return to the LORD, that He may have mercy on him, and to our God, for He will abundantly pardon.
ISAIAH 55:6–7

Return to the LORD, your God,
for He is gracious and merciful,
slow to anger, and abounding in mercy,
and repents of evil.
Who knows whether He will not turn and repent,
and leave a blessing behind Him?
JOEL 2:12–14

If My people who are called by My name humble themselves, and pray and seek My face, and turn from their wicked ways, then I will hear them from heaven, and will forgive their sin and heal their land.
2 CHRONICLES 7:14

t last the Voice fell silent;
the Burden, delivered.

    In the stillness,
a Heartbeat: 920
steady, strong, insistent,
the sound of Love pounding
on the door of the universe,
awaiting a reply.

In the darkness appeared
a blazing Heart
vast as the heavens,
brilliant as the lightning,
Supernova of mercy
whose mighty beams 930
shattered the night.

Among the shards of darkness
was a tiny black hole,
frozen mouth
of a bottomless abyss,
dungeon of the second death.

Before every creature
the choice awaits:

The Brilliance or the blackness;
the Fire or the frost; 940
the Heart or the hole;
the Love or the loss.

Choose now,
in this knowledge:

All flesh is grass.
He blesses, we flourish;
He curses, we wither.
His Love alone lasts.

REPENT

Unless you repent you will ... perish.

LUKE 13:5

PRAY

Pray constantly.

1 THESSALONIANS 5:17

PREPARE

Prepare to meet your God.

AMOS 4:12

WITNESS

You shall be My witnesses.

ACTS 1:8

SCRIPTURAL ALLUSIONS AND PARALLELS

Every tenth line in the text has been identified by a small numeral in the right margin of the page. This arrangement allows the reader to determine each line's number without permitting the numerals to intrude unnecessarily into the text. (Line spaces are not counted.) The index will assist those who wish to know the scriptural references of any given line, to view the extensive biblical context of the work as a whole, and to study more deeply the related passages from Scripture.

Line number	Scriptural text
2	1 Kings 19:12
4–5	Revelation 14:2
6–7	Habakkuk 2:2
8–9	Isaiah 40:6
11–12	Revelation 14:7
13–16	Ezekiel 3:16–19; Isaiah 51:17; 52:1–2
17–18	Isaiah 55:7; Jeremiah 3:22; 15:19
20	Isaiah 47:15
25–31	Isaiah 21:1; 3–4; the Hebrew word in verse 1 and other passages that is often translated as "oracle" or "word" means literally "burden"; see also, for example, Isaiah 13:1; 15:1; 17:1; 19:1; 21:11, 13; 22:1; 23:1; 30:6; Ezekiel 12:10; Nahum 1:1; Habakkuk 1:1; Zechariah 9:1.
32	Isaiah 22:1
33–36	Isaiah 40:6–8
42	Revelation 4:1

Line number	Scriptural text
46	Ezekiel 28:18
48	Genesis 3:19; Psalm 104:29; Ecclesiastes 3:20; Isaiah 25:12
53–56	Psalm 90:4–6
57–60	Job 39:27–30; Jeremiah 49:14–16; Obadiah 2–4
62	Malachi 4:2
75	Isaiah 1:5–6
78	John 1:4–5
80–81	Ezekiel 16:8–15
84–90	Hosea 11:1–4
89–93	Isaiah 17:10–11; Jeremiah 2:32; 3:21–22; 13:25; 18:15–17
94–95	Hosea 13:4–9; Ezekiel 16:49
97	Lamentations 2:3
104–105	Genesis 3:19; Psalm 90:3
108–111	John 3:8; Acts 2:2; John 3:19–21; Isaiah 6:9–12; 42:18; Matthew 13:14–15
112–115	Psalm 83:13–16; 107:25; 148:8; Nahum 1:3
135	Deuteronomy 30:19–20
144–145	Genesis 25:29–34
149–150	Matthew 26:14–16
160–161	Jeremiah 31:15; Matthew 2:16–18
164–166	Proverbs 30:20
167–168	Lamentations 1:12
172–173	Isaiah 66:4
174–176	Jeremiah 10:20
179–180	Genesis 9:5–6
181–182	Genesis 19:24–25
183	Job 38:29–30; 2 Kings 8:1; Psalm 105:16; Isaiah 51:19; Jeremiah 11:22; 15:2–4
185	Isaiah 1:7; 30:30; 47:14; 66:15–16

Line number	Scriptural text
189–204	Exodus chapters 12–14; Galatians 5:9
205–210	Revelation 6:9–11
211–216	Job 20:19–20; 28:13–17; Psalm 10:2–4; Proverbs 22:16; Zechariah 9:3–4; James 2:15–16, 5:1–6; Isaiah 3:15; Deuteronomy 13:11
217–218	Exodus chapter 32; Deuteronomy 9:16–21; Psalm 106:19–22; Exodus 15:10; Jeremiah 6:29
219–228	Proverbs 6:9–11; 12:24; 15:19; 18:9; 19:15, 24; 24:30–34; Ecclesiastes 10:18; 2 Thessalonians 3:7–12
229–236	Proverbs 22:7, 26–27
237–241	Job 22:8; Proverbs 22:7
252–254	Job 27:18–21; Matthew 7:26–27
255–256	Isaiah 30:12–14
257–261	Nahum 3:16–17; Ezekiel 13:13–14
262	Proverbs 10:16
263	Job 37:1–5; Psalm 144:6
264–266	Isaiah 1:22; Ezekiel 7:19; Zephaniah 1:18; Lamentations 4:1
267–270	Lamentations 1:1–3; Isaiah 15:3; 24:7–12; 32:14
275–277	Lamentations 1:11; 2:11–12, 19, 21; 4:4–5, 9
278	Ezekiel 16:39; 23:26
279	Amos 2:4–5
280–282	Job 24:14; Zechariah 11:9; Jeremiah 20:8–9; Isaiah 9:20; Leviticus 26:27–29; Deuteronomy 28:52–57; Lamentations 2:20
283–291	Luke 15:11–24
299–305	Zechariah 11:9; Jeremiah 20:8–9; Isaiah 9:20; Leviticus 26:27–29; Deuteronomy 28:52–57; Lamentations 2:20
306	Isaiah 58:11; Jeremiah 31:12
310	Matthew 13:5–6

Line number	Scriptural text
312	Job 27:22; Isaiah 28:2; Jeremiah 47:2; Nahum 1:8; Matthew 24:37–39
314	Matthew 2:1
315–316	Matthew 15:14
325–331	Ezekiel 27:26–27; 1 Timothy 1:19
332–341	Psalm 58:3–5; 140:1–3; Romans 3:13–18; Matthew 3:7; Luke 3:7
344–345	Isaiah 5:20–21
346–347	2 Chronicles 36:15–16; Isaiah 28:22; Jude 17–18
354–355	Psalm 94:4–11; Isaiah 59:1–8;
356–357	2 Peter 3:3–4, 8–10
359	Hebrews 10:37; Habakkuk 2:3
360	Lamentations 2:10; 3:28–30; Amos 5:13; 8:3; Habakkuk 2:20
372	Proverbs 23:8
374	Psalm 31:18
375–378	Matthew 12:34–37
381–385	Ezekiel chapter 1; Revelation 4:6–8
394	Psalm 10:9; 35:7–8; 140:5; Proverbs 29:5
395	Psalm 91:11
399	Exodus 3:14; Isaiah 47:1–11
400	Proverbs 24:5
401–403	Not a scriptural allusion, but a reference to a celebrated comment by John Emerich Edward Dahlberg Acton (Lord Acton); b. 1834, d. 1902
405–408	Job 8:13–14; Isaiah 59:5–8
409–413	Ezekiel chapter 1; Revelation 4:6–8
414–418	Job 8:13–14; Isaiah 59:5–8
421–422	Matthew 5:11–12
423	Jeremiah 6:16–17; Isaiah 21:6–10; Ezekiel 3:16–21; 33:1–9

Line number	Scriptural text
429	Ezekiel 1:26
431	Exodus 3:14; Deuteronomy 32:39
432	Psalm 41:13; 90:2
435	Isaiah 66:1
437	Psalm 110:1; 1 Corinthians 15:25
438	Numbers 4:15; 1 Chronicles 16:22; Psalm 105:15
439	Job 8:13–14; 27:18; 1 Kings 16:1–3; 21:21
440	Exodus 15:8; 2 Samuel 22:16; Job 4:9; Psalm 18:15
442	Genesis 19:11; Deuteronomy 28:28–29; 2 Kings 6:18; Isaiah 29:9; Zephaniah 1:14–17; Ezekiel 6:9; Job 11:20; 36:30—37:13; 2 Samuel 22:14–15; Psalm 144:6; Zechariah 9:14; Revelation 4:5
443	Ezekiel 22:17–22; Genesis 19:28; Matthew 13:41–42, 49–50; Exodus 32:10; Numbers 16:35; Job 19:11; 42:7; Psalm 79:5; 89:46; Jeremiah 4:4; 21:12
444	Daniel 12:3; Matthew 13:43
445	John 17:22; Romans 2:9–10; 5:2; 8:18; 2 Corinthians 3:18; 4:17; Colossians 1:27; 3:4; 2 Thessalonians 2:14; 1 Peter 5:1, 4; 2 Peter 1:3
446ff	Hosea 5:4; Revelation 17:1–6
465ff	Deuteronomy 23:17–18; 1 Kings 14:22–24; Romans 1:24–32
470	Proverbs 11:6; Isaiah 57:5; Jeremiah 2:23–25; 5:7–9; Jude 7
472–474	Revelation 14:8; 18:1–24
475	Romans 6:16; Galatians 4:8–9; Titus 3:3; 2 Peter 2:17–19
476	Revelation 18:23
485	Revelation 18:24
493–497	Revelation 18:20–24
504–510	Isaiah 3:4–5, 12; 30:1; 57:4; Jeremiah 4:22; Matthew 11:16–17

Line number	Scriptural text
511	1 Corinthians 13:11
517	Matthew 11:16
526–530	Isaiah 34:11–15
532–536	Job 5:17–18; Psalm 39:11; 94:12–13; Proverbs 16:22; Jeremiah 2:19; Lamentations 4:6; 1 Corinthians 11:22; Revelation 3:19
536	1 Corinthians 13:11
544ff	Malachi 1:3
547–548	Matthew 9:34; 10:25; 12:24–27; Mark 3:22; Luke 11:15–19; Ephesians 2:2
549	Exodus 8:21–24; Psalm 78:45; 105:31
551	Job 16:9; Psalm 35:16; 37:12–13; Lamentations 2:16
552	Revelation 13:5–7; Leviticus 7:27; Psalm 10:7–8; Zechariah 9:7
556	Matthew 25:32–33
557	Isaiah 17:10–11; 65:22; Amos 5:11
558	Exodus 10:3–20
559–562	Job 19:15; Psalm 41:9; John 13:18
563–564	Jeremiah 6:14
570	Isaiah 41:29; Jeremiah 10:15; 21:18; 51:18; 2 Thessalonians 2:9–12
572–573	Revelation 6:1–8; Psalm 33:17; Isaiah 31:1
579	Psalm 76:5; Ezekiel 16:39; 23:26–27; Hosea 2:3
583–586	Romans 9:32–33; 10:11; 1 Peter 2:7–8; Isaiah 28:16; Daniel 2:44–45; Psalm 118:22–23; Matthew 21:42; Acts 4:11
590–591	Revelation 6:12; Joel 2:31; Acts 2:20; Ezekiel 32:7; Matthew 24:29; Isaiah 13:10; Malachi 4:2
596	Isaiah 56:9–11
599–603	Psalm 23
604	Jeremiah 25:34

Line number	Scriptural text
605	Deuteronomy 6:10–12; 8:11–20; 32:18; Psalm 9:17; Judges 3:7–8
606	Psalm 14:1–3; 119:118; Isaiah 53:6; Jeremiah 50:6; Hosea 4:12; Amos 2:14; Romans 3:10–12; Hebrews 3:10–11
607	Psalm 119:21; Jeremiah 14:10; Zechariah 10:2; 1 Timothy 6:10
608	Hosea 5:11
609	1 Samuel 8:7
610	Psalm 12:1; Nehemiah 1:8
611–612	Jeremiah 12:10–11; Ezekiel 32:2; 34:18–19
616	John 10:12–13
617	John 3:19–21; Isaiah 6:9–12; 42:18; Matthew 13:14–15
618	Matthew 25:32–33
620	Jeremiah 10:21; 23:1–2; Ezekiel 34:5–6; Nahum 3:18
621	Ecclesiastes 2:10–11; Isaiah 58:13; Luke 8:14; 2 Timothy 3:4; Titus 3:3
624	Isaiah 13:21
626–629	Jeremiah 13:15–17
630–635	Psalm 7:2; 17:12; 22:13; Jeremiah 2:30; 4:7; 5:6; 50:6–7; Ezekiel 22:25, 27; Zephaniah 3:3; 1 Peter 5:8–11; Hosea 8:1; Zephaniah 2:14; Proverbs 30:17; Lamentations 4:19; Revelation 9:3–10; Ezekiel 2:6; Luke 10:19; Isaiah 17–18
636–644	Matthew 7:15; Acts 20:28–31; Ezekiel 34:20–22
645–650	Revelation 7:13–17
651	An allusion, not to Scripture, but to the oft-quoted observation of the second-century Christian writer Tertullian that "the blood of Christians is seed."
652–654	Ezra 9:8, 15; Isaiah 10:21–22; Jeremiah 23:3

Line number	Scriptural text
655–658	Jeremiah 3:15; 23:4; Ezekiel 34:11–16; Psalm 27:5; 31:20; 64:2; 91:1–6; Isaiah 51:16; Matthew 16:18
659–660	Psalm 26:2; Jeremiah 9:7; Zechariah 13:9; Malachi 3:2–3; James 1:2–4, 12; 1 Peter 1:6–7; 4:12–13; 2 Peter 2:9; Revelation 2:10
661	Exodus 20:7; Deuteronomy 5:11
662	1 Samuel 15:23; Psalm 68:6; 78:17; Proverbs 17:11; Isaiah 1:28; Jeremiah 28:16; Ezekiel 2:3;
663–666	Matthew 7:22–23; 8:12; 13:24–42; 22:13; 25:30, 41–46; Luke 13:24–28
668–669	Isaiah 19:14; 22:5; 34:11; Micah 7:4
670	2 Kings 21:9; 2 Chronicles 33:9; Daniel 11:32
674–683	Proverbs 30:12; Isaiah 28:8; 30:2–14; 47:15; Jeremiah 10:21; 12:10–11; 23:1–2; 25:34–38; 30:6–7; Ezekiel 22:15; 24:13; 34:1–10; Matthew 15:14; 23:16–22; Jude 13
684–689	John 10:12–13
690–697	Ezekiel 34:10
698–700	John 10:11
701–704	Psalm 23
705–706	2 Timothy 4:8; James 1:12; 1 Peter 5:4; Revelation 2:10; 3:11
707–708	Jeremiah 23:11
709–713	Psalm 22:12–13, 16, 19–21;
715	Matthew 16:18–19
716–722	Job 27:20–23; Psalm 69:2, 15; 88:15–17; Jonah 2:5
723–724	Exodus 3:14; 1 Kings 19:11–12; Psalm 32:6–7; Psalm 57:1; 107:28–30; 124:1–5
725	Ephesians 6:13
726	Luke 22:31–32
727	Matthew 6:12–15; Luke 6:37; 23:34; Ephesians 4:32; Colossians 3:13

Line number	Scriptural text
728–729	Matthew 10:38; 16:24–25; Mark 8:31–37; Luke 9:23–24; 1 Peter 2:21
730	Matthew 16:18
731–739	John 21:18–19; Psalm 22:6–8; 12–18
740	Psalm 22:1; Matthew 27:46; Mark 15:34
741–742	Psalm 31:5; Luke 23:46
743–745	Acts 7:54–60
746	Revelation 2:26–28; 22:16; 2 Peter 1:19; Romans 13:14
747	Revelation 8:10–11
748	Revelation 12:3–4, 9; Psalm 59:5
749–750	Psalm 9:5; 94:10; Micah 7:16–17; 1 Peter 4:7
751–753	Matthew 17:3; 24:29–33; 27:51–53; Mark 9:4; 2 Maccabees 15:12–16
754–761	Matthew 24:6–8, 21–22, 29–30; Numbers 16:41–50; Psalm 106:29; Zechariah 14:12; Jeremiah 15:2–4; 24:10
762–763	Ezekiel 28:18; Genesis 3:19; Psalm 104:29; Ecclesiastes 3:20; Isaiah 25:12
764–769	Amos 8:9–10; Isaiah 43:14; Lamentations 5:15; James 4:9
772	Genesis 9:11–17
773	Isaiah 1:7; 30:30; 47:14; 66:15–16; 2 Peter 3:5–7, 10
774–775	Isaiah 51:17, 22; Jeremiah 25:15–17; Ezekiel 23:32–34; Revelation 14:9–10
776–778	Jeremiah 25:29
779–780	Ecclesiastes 4:2; Jeremiah 22:10; Revelation 9:6; 14:13
781–783	Revelation 2:10; 3:11; 5:9; 14:6; 2 Timothy 4:8; James 1:12; 1 Peter 5:4
784–794	Romans 8:18–23

Line number	Scriptural text
795–801	Genesis 1:14–18; Job 9:9–10; 38:4–7, 31–33; Psalm 19:1–6; 136:4–9; Isaiah 48:13
802–808	Revelation 12:1–2, 5
809	Luke 1:28
810–812	Revelation 12:2; Romans 8:19–22
813–820	Luke 1:46–55
816	John 12:38; Psalm 77:15; 89:10; Isaiah 30:30–32; 33:2; 40:10; 51:9; 52:10; 53:1; 59:16; 63:5; Jeremiah 21:5; 27:5; 32:17–19; Ezekiel 20:33–38 (and many others)
817–818	Genesis 11:1–9; Psalm 2:1–4; 68:1; 92:9
819	Isaiah 10:13; 14:3–20
820	Job 5:11; 22:29; Psalm 149:4; Proverbs 3:34; 29:23; James 4:6, 10; 1 Peter 5:5–6; 2 Timothy 2:11–13; Revelation 3:21; 20:4; 22:5
822–825	Revelation 12:1
828–833	Genesis 3:13–15; Revelation 12:3–9; 20:1–3; Psalm 91:13
838–839	Matthew 27:45; Mark 15:33; Luke 22:53; 23:44–45; Ephesians 6:12; Philippians 2:14–16; 1 John 2:8, 18
840–841	Psalm 18:7; 60:2–3; 68:7–8; 99:1; Isaiah 5:25; 6:4; 24:19–20; 64:1–3; Ezekiel 31:16; 38:20; Nahum 1:5; Hebrews 12:26–27; Matthew 27:51–54; 28:2; Revelation 6:12–17; 8:5; 11:13, 19; 16:18–21; Exodus 19:18; Judges 5:5; 2 Samuel 22:8
842–843	Matthew 24:35–36; Mark 13:32–37; Luke 12:40, 46; Acts 1:6–7; Revelation 3:3
844–847	Matthew 24:27–31; Luke 9:29; 17:24; 21:27; 1 Thessalonians 4:16; 1 Corinthians 15:23, 51–57; 2 Thessalonians 2:1; Acts 1:9–11; Zephaniah 1:14–18; Job 36:30—37:13; Psalm 105:32; 144:6; Zechariah 9:14; Revelation 1:7; 4:5; Daniel 10:6; Colossians 3:4

Line number	Scriptural text
848	Matthew 3:12; 13:30, 36–43; 24:30–31; 25:31–33; Mark 13:26–27; John 11:51–52; 2 Thessalonians 2:1
849–850	Ezekiel 37:11–14; John 5:21, 28–29; 6:38–40, 44, 54; 11:25; Romans 6:5–11; 1 Corinthians 6:14; 15:12–58; 2 Corinthians 4:14; Revelation 20:12
851	Revelation 20:13
852–855	Psalm 19:1–4; 148:1–4, 13;
856–857	Hebrews 4:13; Job 26:6; Daniel 7:9–10; Amos 2:16; Psalm 82:8; 96:13; Isaiah 33:22; Matthew 25:31–46; John 5:22—29; 2 Timothy 4:1; Hebrews 10:30; 1 Peter 1:17; 4:5; Revelation 11:18
858–859	Matthew 10:26; Mark 4:22–23; Luke 8:17; 12:2–3; Romans 2:16; 1 Corinthians 4:5; Ephesians 5:11–13
860–861	Romans 2:5–8; Matthew 25:31–46; Mark 12:36–37
864–867	Revelation 4:6; 15:2; 1 Corinthians 13:12
868–875	Ecclesiastes 3:11; Isaiah 40:5, 25–31; 41:4; 46:8–10; Ephesians 2:10
876–878	Ezekiel 36:23; 39:26–27; Philippians 2:9–11; Psalm 51:4
879–880	Hebrews 12:29
881	Psalm 21:8–9; Ezekiel 22:20–22; Malachi 4:1; Matthew 13:41–43, 49
882	Proverbs 17:3; 1 Corinthians 3:12–15; Malachi 3:2–3
883–884	John 17:22; Romans 5:2; 8:18; 9:23; 2 Corinthians 3:18; 4:17; Colossians 3:4; 2 Thessalonians 2:14; Hebrews 2:10; 1 Peter 5:1, 4; 2 Peter 1:3; Revelation 21:1–11, 23
885–893	Revelation 6:12–14; 21:1; Joel 2:30–31; Acts 2:19–20; Ezekiel 32:7–8; Matthew 24:29; Isaiah 13:9–10; 24:23; Malachi 4:2

Line number	Scriptural text
894–895	Genesis 3:13–15; Revelation 12:9; 19:20; 20:1–3, 13–15; Isaiah 24:21–22
896–897	Matthew 4:1; 6:13; Mark 1:13; Luke 4:13; 1 Corinthians 7:5; 1 Thessalonians 3:5; Revelation 12:10; 20:10; Job 1:9–11; Daniel 11:32; Genesis 3:13; John 8:44; 2 John 7; 2 Corinthians 11:3
898–899	Revelation 14:9–11
900–901	Isaiah 5:16–17; 40:11; Revelation 5:6–14; 7:17; 12:11; 17:14; 19:7–9; 21:6, 21; 22:1–5, 17; John 4:10–15; 7:37–39; Isaiah 12:3; 35:7; 41:18; 43:19–21; 49:10; 58:11; Jeremiah 2:13; 17:13; Ezekiel 47:1–12
902–903	Daniel 7:18; 1 Peter 5:5–6; 2 Timothy 2:12; Revelation 3:21; 20:4; 22:5
904–905	Revelation 4:4–11; 5:8–10; 14:1–3; 15:1–4
906–909	Revelation 4:8; Isaiah 6:3
910	Revelation 19:7–9; 21:1–4; 22:17; Matthew 9:14–15; 25:1–13; Mark 2:18–20; Luke 5:33–35; John 3:25–30; 2 Corinthians 1:2; Ephesians 5:31–32; Song of Solomon 1:2–4; 2:4, 10; 7:10; Isaiah 61:10; 62:5
911	Revelation 10:6 (Douay Rheims Version); 2 Peter 3:18
912–916	Exodus 3:14; Isaiah 41:4; John 8:58; Revelation 1:8, 17; 21:6
919–921	Jeremiah 31:20; Matthew 11:29; Song of Solomon 4:9
932–934	Revelation 3:20
935–936	Revelation 9:1–2, 11; 11:7; 17:8; 20:1–3, 6, 14–15; 21:08; John 8:51; Isaiah 14:15; 42:7; Ezekiel 26:20–21; 32:23; 1 Corinthians 15:26, 54–57
937–938	Deuteronomy 30:15–20; Joshua 24:14–15; Hebrews 12:25

Line number	Scriptural text
943–944	Deuteronomy 30:15–20; Joshua 24:14–15; Hebrews 12:25
945–947	Isaiah 40:6–8
948	Jeremiah 31:1–3; 1 Corinthians 13:8; Psalm 136

ABOUT THE AUTHOR

Paul Thigpen, Ph.D., is an award-winning journalist and best-selling author. Among his most popular titles are *The Rapture Trap* (Ascension, 2001) and the novel *My Visit to Hell* (Realms, 2007).

Dr. Thigpen's writing reflects a wide variety of genres and subjects: history and biography, spirituality and apologetics, anthologies and devotionals, family life and children's books, study guides and reference works, fiction and collections of poetry and prayers. In addition to the forty books he has authored or compiled, he has published more than five hundred journal, magazine, and newsletter articles in more than forty religious and secular periodicals for both scholarly and popular audiences. His work has been circulated worldwide and translated into twelve languages.

A 1977 *summa cum laude* graduate of Yale University (in Religious Studies), Dr. Thigpen was awarded the George W. Woodruff Fellowship at Emory University, where he earned an M.A. (1993) and a Ph.D. (1995) in Historical Theology. In 1993 he was named as a Jacob K. Javits Fellow by the U.S. Department of Education. He has since served on the theology faculties of several universities and colleges and is currently the editor of TAN Books, based in Charlotte, North Carolina.

Notes

Notes

NOTES

Made in the USA
San Bernardino, CA
11 December 2015